MW00990330

# WITHDRAWN

**Please check all items for damages
before leaving the Library.
Thereafter you will be held
responsible for all injuries
to items beyond reasonable wear.**

| 9/13
| 11/15

## Helen M. Plum Memorial Library

### Lombard, Illinois

A daily fine will be charged for
overdue materials.

DEC    2012

Time of Useful Consciousness

Lawrence Ferlinghetti

# *Time of Useful Consciousness*
## (*Americus, Book II*)

A NEW DIRECTIONS BOOK

811
FER

Manufactured in the United States of America
New Directions Books are printed on acid-free paper.
First published as a New Directions Book in 2012
Published simultaneously in Canada by Penguin Books Canada Limited
Design by Erik Rieselbach

*Library of Congress Cataloging in Publication Data*
Ferlinghetti, Lawrence.
Time of useful consciousness / Lawrence Ferlinghetti.
p. cm.
"Americus, Book II."
ISBN 978-0-8112-2031-6
1. National characteristics, American—Poetry. 2. United States—Poetry. I. Title.
PS3511.E557T56 2012
811'.54—dc23

2012014082


10 9 8 7 6 5 4 3 2 1

New Directions Books are published for James Laughlin
by New Directions Publishing Corporation
80 Eighth Avenue, New York 10011

3 1502 00754 5427

for Nancy Joyce Peters

# I.

In that hinternation
that stretches westward from Manhattan
autumn finds the people restless
Across the iron cities
cement plains and silted rivers
Across Appalachia
Across Ohio
(first western frontier)
And down into it
down into middle America
hinter America
by Great Lakes yearning
by Firelands burning
Redbrick mansions moldering
down the wooded streets
of a hundred winded towns
Under the huge sugar maples
down the canyons of dying leaves
each a hand letting go
in the full catastrophe
the full miracle of life …

Homer heard it
by the Aegean long ago
by the ocean's long withdrawing roar
the cry of the voyager
always outward bound
over bright horizons
to new worlds

And then seeking home again
steering toward democracy
even as they plundered everywhere
and took slaves wherever

And we had our own town criers—
Whitman Melville Emerson Thoreau
Thomas Paine and Mark Twain
And Thomas Wolfe
with his destiny that leads
to the soft stone smile of an angel
in lives "haunted by a Georgia slattern
because a London cut-purse went unhung"
And Woody Guthrie and Dylan
and Pete Seeger and Johnny Cash
and Paul Robeson singing "Joe Hill"—
the true popular poets of America
their voices moving everyone
(more than the poets in books,
the printing press having made them so silent)

But all of them, singing or silent,
reading between the lines

reading between the lives of America—
Packs of players facing West
the Jacks and Queens of Hearts
on Mercator maps of America
the black-eyed ones who see all ways
the one with the eye of a horse
the one with the light in his eye
the one with his eye on the star named Nova
the one for the ones with no one to lead them
the one whose day has just begun
the one with the star in his cap
the cat with future feet
looking like a Jack of Hearts
Mystic Jack Zen Jack with crazy koans
Vegas Jack who rolls the bones
the high roller behind the dealer
the one who'll shake them
the one who'll shake the ones unshaken
the fearless one
the one without bullshit
the stud with the straightest answer
the one with blazing words for guns
the distance runner with the word to pass
the night rider with the urgent message
The man from La Mancha riding bareback
The one who bears the great tradition
and breaks it
The Mysterious Stranger who comes & goes
The Jack or Queen of Hearts who speaks out
The Fast Speaking Woman
and the Slow Speaking Woman

the one who digs the mystery
and stands in the corner smiling
like a Jack or Queen of Hearts
like Big Jack Groovy Jack the Jack of Light
Sainted Jack who had the Revelations
and spoke the poem of apocalypse
Poet Jack with the light pack
who travels by himself
and leaves the ladies smiling
Dharma Jack with the beatitudes
drunk on a bus addressing everyone
the silent ones with the frozen faces
the ones with *The Wall Street Journal*
who never speak to strangers
the ones that got lost in the shuffle
and never drew the Jack of Hearts
the one who'd turn them on
who'd save them from themselves
the one who heals the Hamlet in them
the silent Ham who never acts
the dude on the corner in two-tone shoes
who knows the name of the game
and names his game
the kid who paints the fence
the boy who digs the treasure up
the boy with the beans on the beanstalk
the dandy man the candy man
the one with the lollipops
the harlequin man
who tells the tic-toc man to stuff it
in front of the house that Jack built

behind the house that Jack built
where sleeps the Cock that crowed in the morn
where sleeps the Cow with the crumpled horn
where sleeps the Dude who kept the Horse
with the beautiful form
and kissed the Maiden all forlorn
the Jack of the pack all tattered and torn
the one the Queen keeps her eye on
Dark Rider on a white horse
Prophet stoned on the wheel of fortune
Sweet singer with harp half-hid
who speaks with the cry of cicadas
who tells the tale too truly
the true tale of sound and fury
the Jack of Hearts who lays it out
who tells it as it is
the one who wears no watch
yet tells the time too truly
and reads the Knight of Cups
and knows himself
the Knave of Hearts the Jack of Hearts
who stole the tarts
of love & laughter
the Jack who tells his dream
to the hard-eyed innocents
and lays it out for the blind hippie
the black dream the white dream
of the Jack of Hearts
whose skeleton is neither black nor white
the long dream the dream of heads & hearts
the trip of hearts the flip of hearts

that turns the Hanged Man right side up
and saves the Drowned Sailor
with the breath of love
the wet dream the hard dream the sweet dream
of the Deck Hand on the tall ship sailing softly
Blackjack yellowjack the steeplejack
who sets the clock in the tower
and sees the chimes of freedom flashing
his only watch within him
the high one the turned-on one the tuned-in one
the one who digs
and finds the sun-stone
of himself
the woman-man
who holds all worlds together
when all is said and all is done
in the wild eye the wide eye
of the Jack of Hearts
who stands in a doorway
clothed in sun …

# II.

So that—sailing westward
from the crenellated old world
of over-age Camembert Europe—
millions washing up on virgin shores
bright with promise

"Awake and sing, ye who dwell in the dust!"

Ideas alphabets fornications
Transmigrations transgressions
Roman noses blown in Sephardic profiles
Arab lips praising Allah in Alabama
   *Al illaha il allah All illaha il allah*
Prayer rugs traded
for status symbols in Cincinnati
Baseballs lost among the Pleiades (quoth Lamantia)
Boris & Bessie Thomashefsky
born Yiddish in the Ukraine
spawning the genius maestro MTT
("You're not in the shtetl anymore, baby")

And birth certificates
for the first-born of immigrant families
inscribed with names like *Americus d'Alessandro*

And not all pure heroes
as various villains show up too
and various home-grown bourgeois fascists
and defacers of the Statue of Liberty
(*"Don't* give me your tired, your poor,
your huddled masses....")
And they shipped out
Russian-born Emma Goldman and Alexander Berkman
back to where they came from

America America!
"stranger than paradise"
to a Hungarian immigrant named Jarmusch
who in his amazement
made a film about it

And old hunchback Tony Tenori
Genovese fisherman
smelling of garlic and pepperoni
catching crayfish in the Bronx River
off Parkway Road Bronxville
where he lived in a hut by the railroad tracks
where sometimes could be heard
the sweet sad sound of the mandolin

And Gregorio Nunzio Corso
born Calabrese orphan on Bleecker Street

who became a poet in prison
mouthing mad mouthfuls of new American lingo

And French canuck Jack Kerouac
growing up American in Lowell Mass.
a Red Sox fan in his lumberjack shirt
speaking *joual* with Mémère
his Quebecoise mother

And Delia Devine fled to America
from the last Great Irish Potato Famine
ending up as housekeeper
in a fine mansion in Westchester
still speaking her rough Irish brogue
And a sharp tongue she had
and fast on the uptake she was
with the wit of her publican father
downing his fifth pint

While millions of blacks uprooted out of Africa
deprived of homes and names
enslaved in the Deep South
finally escape to a larger America
to make a name for themselves

While W.E.B. Du Bois born in Great Barrington Mass. by a Dutch-
African mother and a father descended from West African slaves
grew up to write *The Souls of Black Folk*
striking like a thunderclap
on the ears of those who didn't want to hear it

And Catholic Jack Powers in Boston
who never would go West
born Black Irish in Roxbury projects
fed the poor from throwaways
at the Public Market
and made poetry out of Stone Soup and beer
all those years
then lost babbling in a psycho room
in Mass. General
   *Where now*
     *Brother poet . . . ?*
He was an American
He was an American boy
He read the Reader's Digest from cover to cover
and noted the close identification of America
and the promised Land
He read the Want Ads daily
looking for a stone a leaf an unfound door
He wandered lonely as a cloud
He heard the sound of summer in the rain ...
He leaned in drunken doorways
He heard America singing
in the Yellow Pages
where one could never tell
the soul has its rages

And all he had known
was sown inside him
and morphed in memories of dreams

All those immigrants
melded into one new man
a new *brand* of man—
The old guy in shirt sleeves with arm bands
on vacation back in the Old Country
(his first time back in thirty years
and he looks around dazed)
And the Polish lady on Fifth Avenue
parking her Mercedes in her private garage
And the kid in short pants on his skateboard
And the old dame
wiping the counter of the diner
in South Side Chicago
And the old codger in baggy pants
playing chess in Washington Square
And the prom queen from the South
about to enter Columbia College
and major in Men
And the cabinet maker in Connecticut
who just lost his wife to cancer
screaming in the dark
Even as Babette Deutsch tells her class at Columbia
"How can we write the great Russian novel
while life goes on so unterribly?"

And so on and on
around the bend of our river
steering toward democracy
to write the history of the future
in the sweep of history's broken broom

as history goes on repeating itself
and every war and every execution
a defeat for the people
And Sacco & Vanzetti rocking the nation
as they fried in wooden electric chairs

With other immigrants creating caustic critiques
of the American Way of Life
like Noam Chomsky
with a father from the Ukraine
and a mother from Belarus
or Howard Zinn rewriting history and herstory
with a father from Austria-Hungary
and a mother from Siberia

For Hitler had shaken the tree
and the full fruit of Euro brains
fell on America
Barzun and other polyglots at Columbia U.
Einstein walking with Gödel
down Princeton's leafy lanes
French Surrealist refugees
conning Manhattan galleristas
and Easterners listening
to Mahler's fatal forebodings
and Westerners to country-western
(folk music in overdrive)
Back when heartland America
was still all small towns

with small town life the only life
before the Iron Horse came on shining rails
steering toward democracy
and linked them all together
possibly as a nation

As in Clarksville Tennessee in MARY'S HUNGRY CORNER at
the intersection of Legion and North First Street in an ancient two
story brick building next to the LEGION ST. BLUE GRASS
HALL just off the public square above the Cumberland River.
The sign on the door says OPEN SIX A.M. OR WHENEVER
MARY GETS HERE. Inside the creaky door four little men in
overalls at a wooden table are yakking and drinking coffee. There
are three more little men at another old table near the back. They
all look beat-up. You can hear their drawls. There's a little beat-up
counter with stools and a handwritten sign on a soft drink cooler
that reads NO ONE AT BAR. The 200-pound woman who must
be Mary is behind this counter wearing a floppy flowered blouse
and white shoes and hollering at the men at the front table.
"I told him if I took him home I'd straighten out his back!" she
hollers, "I didn't know he was that drunk—"
Three of the men guffaw. The fourth gets up real slow without
straightening up all the way and stands there swaying and crooning
to himself a snatch of bluegrass tune.
Big Mary turns her eyes on a stranger sitting off in a corner.
"Got any grits?" he asks her.
"Nobody ain't ask for any lately."
But she ducks behind the counter and comes up with some and
shoves it into a little electric oven.

"What you want with it—milk or butter?"

"Butter."

She gives him a strange look. "You from 'round here?"

"I'm heading Out West on the next freight. No matter where I's from."

*And suddenly he starts crying.*

Heading west a state of mind
moving west by myriad rutted routes
where a man can stake as much land
as he can ride across before sundown
foraging the far horizon
for the ultimate Eldorado
including Dust Bowl Okies and Tom Joad
trampling down his Grapes of Wrath with words
"Wherever they's a fight so hungry people can eat
I'll be there.
Whenever they's a cop beatin' up a guy, I'll be there…."

# III.

Dark mind dark soul dark age
A man made of steel
on a horse of gold
and the horse hitched to a prairie wagon

East of Santa Fe you can still see from a small plane
the old wagon tracks in the earth
ruts a mile wide
You can almost hear the cracks of whips over horses
the cries of drivers in the dust

And the barren highlands
the desert barrens
where nothing moves
when the west wind blows
not even the cactus
except for the tumbleweeds
like rootless men
rolling along
whichever way the wind blows

The white dawns bursting
over mesas and table lands

Onward by any wheel or horse
any rail any car
by buggy by stagecoach
walking riding
hooves pounding the Great Plains
caravans in the night!

Horizons of mesas
like plains of Spain high up
in Don Quixote country
Sharp eroded towers of bluffs
like windmills tilted
Great long rectangular stone islands
sticking up on far plains
like forts or cargo ships
high on plains of water
Sunset and strange clouds like islands
rayed with light from below
Wagon trains full of families
disappearing in blizzards

And Lewis & Clark on their expedition
shoving off from Saint Louis
in long boats loaded with loneliness
(and good will and greed)
Up the Missouri and West
(retraced in 2004 by a grandson)
Greeted with friendliness by the Lakota

(And the polite response of later Pale Faces
to cut off the hands held out to them)

"Go West young man
and grow up with the country!"
The great treks west
A sea of people on the move
steering toward democracy
Horses mules & oxen
covered wagons buggies carts
filled with all ages
yearning for a homestead a home
to grow a family
to grow enough to eat
in the hard land
in the hard winters in the frozen wastes
with sickness and death en route
Doldrums dreams hallucinations
Conscience and consciousness
of a newborn nation
half-mumbled in sleep
Rocking
restless to the last horizon

Trains in the night!
Shuttles … freights …
Boxcars boxcars boxcars
The first Iron Horses
hooting lonely in the great dark
across still open prairies
connecting isolate towns

connecting everyone for the first time
sprawled across the continent

A race to the West
bypassing Buffalo
once the Athens of America
the great railhead
for all freight heading across
through the Erie Canal
to the Great Lakes and on
Buffalo and the Last Good Time Bar in its glory days

And the cry of "Gold!"
and the Gold Rush and the Forty-Niners
and the great escape westward from the Civil War
(Samuel Clemens becoming Mark Twain in California)
and Henry Ford's Model A's and Model T's
making roads as they went
"Every day Independence day
to him who owns a Ford"
and Henry himself driving off
in a dense cloud of unknowing
into a dubious immortality
having sown the iron seeds
of Autogeddon
(and no signs yet saying
GO BACK/WRONG WAY)

Onward and Inward!
Seeking and finding
and moving on

Dreams of treasure
nightmares of loss
(Grandpa lost his lone stake
in an imaginary gold mine)
seeking the infinite the absolute happiness
steering for democracy
or whatever glitters

Before the great metal bird
changed the face of the continent
changed the landscape of America—
an America shrunk to an island
seen from forty thousand feet
(the back of a turtle)
Isolate cabins in rock wastes
lonely tracks lost in wilderness mountains
Blips on the screen attesting to
the huge loneliness of the great spaces

The forward rush of time and history
and of this poem
into what future
blessed or blasted
history and herstory
made of the lies of the victors
written in blood and water
in rivers in railroads in highways
in rear-view mirrors
in which the past disappeared faster and faster
like train tracks behind a train speeding-up
and the future unfolding in a windshield

Life sweeping on
The blasts and spins of chance
splitting people up
walking or running or standing still
ever toward or away from each other
further and further away
as old age advances
Old friends or lovers once so close
now stick figures in the distance
disappearing
over the horizon
waving back
*Goodbye! Goodbye!*

Initials in cement in a sidewalk
enclosed in a heart
or in the bark of an ancient tree

*Obsessively remembering*
    *a summer of cicadas*
   *Under the great trees*
      *where the crickets were*
        *Suddenly she stopt laughing*
     *put his hands upon her breasts*

And the trees cut down
Old stone to new high rises
for an omnivorous advancing population
with blind lust and the lonely itch for love—

While on moonlit spring nights
birdsongs
all day and all night
issue from the syrinx
of the northern mockingbird
with two hundred vocalizations
including calls of frogs insects and car alarms
(All all cries of love or cries of despair?)

*A ringing in the air*
*a ringing in the ear*
*a whirring and a sound of winging*
*as of a million birds together singing*
*in the upper air*
*far off echoing—*

And the territorial imperative
 or the testosterone imperative
the selfish gene the selfish id
driving all before it
in the absence of some other motive
some undiscovered mover & shaker
like love—
out where the tall corn grows
every stalk a phallus
sowing sperm broadside …

# IV.

To Chicago! Chicago!
by coach or Pullman or boxcar—
Shantytowns  brick hovels  hotels
palaces built with hogs—

> *In O'Hare Airport*
> *The moving walkway moves along*
> *And, having stopped, moves on*
> *Nor all your piety nor all your wit*
> *Can cancel out a mile of it*

Airport to downtown by Blue Line train. rocking on trestles through elevated stations in the hard rain, through neighborhoods of old Chicago, stockyards far off drowned in the gloaming, grey skies lowering over wet tar roofs, slate roofs on brick buildings, the grey rain pouring down on grey station platforms, grey trees blowing in the slight wind, mute citizens aboard looking tired and bored, October and they already have their winter parkas on, staring at somewhere out the moving windows, life rocking on as if nothing ever happens yet happens to fall on them, here now, the

hard rain catching them full on, two guys on a roof patching a leak
with tar paper, chimney stacks of Old Town, a steeple or two, old
leaning telephone poles with ancient tangled wires, a kid with a
skateboard by the Turkish Russian Baths, a black guy in a win-
dow seat snoozing, wooden porches all along on the backs of brick
houses backed-up to the tracks. The airline stewardess continues
to read. It's a thriller she's reading. The killer with unfed heart is
about to escape and rape her.... Downtown traffic hung up behind
a candy-stripe red-and-white cement truck with its mixer rotating
with a sign reading FIND A HOLE AND FILL IT and no one
in the cab. ... *Chicago, Chicago, Chicago's a helluva town ...*


Hog caller and boomtown of the great farm states
" way out there where the tall corn grows"
where the Populists sprang up in the 1890s
an agrarian populist revolt
with stump speakers shouting "Wall Street owns the country!"
echoing down to today


And on Near North Side Chicago
in a shack of a barn in broken-down Tooker Alley
the Dil Pickle Club (with one "l")
the hobohemian nightspot
after its glorious beginnings
in 1916 or thereabouts
didn't close 'til the 1960s
a place where everybody and everything was *anti*
"the flaming crater of Chicago's revolution in the Arts"
frequented early-on by the likes of
Big Bill Haywood Eugene Debs Emma Goldman
and Mother Jones

Where all the *isms* of the day were fomented or tormented
It was Dil Pickle Dada against the mainstream whitestream
and they were willing to croak for it
for the love of dissent and no government
and total individual freedom
(and Albert Parsons hung at Haymarket for it)

The jazz-age Pickle populated for starters by Wobblies, old Haymarket rads, Bughouse Square soapboxers, anarcho-pacifists, newshounds and booksellers and lecturers on serious subjects, con artists and cops, hoodlums on the lam and pols on the make, prostitutes and printers, infamous poets and novelists who generated the Prairie Renaissance (a rebirth without a prior birth) with Margaret Anderson and Jane Heap and *The Little Review* and Harriet Monroe and *Poetry* and Vachel Lindsay and his "fat black bucks in a wine barrel room" and Carl Sandburg ("The People, Yes!") and Edgar Lee Masters and Ben Hecht and Sherwood Anderson, all leading to James T. Farrell John Dos Passos Nelson Algren and Studs Terkel, with Eugene Debs saying "The master class has always declared the wars, the subject class has always fought the battles"—for which he got ten years in the slammer but told the judge "While there is a lower class I am in it, while there is a criminal element, I am of it, while there is a soul in prison, I am not free."

*As Thorsten Veblen drank the bitter drink alright*

Chicago,Chicago, the city on the make, the lovely lady with a broken nose, quoth Nelson Algren, and he a connoisseur of dames (to wit, his raw letters to Simone de Beauvoir in existential Paris his heirs won't allow to be seen)

Whereas on Pearl Harbor Day 1941 the All American Boy found
himself marching up Michigan Avenue in a tight platoon, wearing
bell bottom trousers ...

Don't let me crowd you
laughs the Irish dame to the sailor
in that Rush Street bar
Chicago 1941
practically sitting down
on top of him
in the booth
while Dinah Washington belts out her blues

Ah been at sea too long
sez he
Yer a long way from the sea
says the Rose of Tralee
Would ya like to taste my salt?
sez he

    *Love me tender,*
        *love me true*
            *All my dreams fulfill*
      *For you know I love you love you*
            *And I always will*

    The sun, the sun also rises over the Loop, burning off the
fog from Lake Michigan, resplendent over squalor. On the stoops
they're still putting out the cans filled with last night's throw-ups.
On Michigan Avenue the huge shining cars start up. A janitor with
his mop and pail steps out a side door of the old redbrick Red Star
Inn and squints at the sun as if he's not seen it before. A whore

crosses over and winks at him like in old-timey movies, hat over one eye. He eyes her and hitches his stiff pants, and she does a Mae West and sez "Is that a flashlight in yer pocket or do ya really love me?" Along Lake Shore Drive the sun glints on statues arrested in time, leaving question marks on their faces. The winter wind off Lake Michigan sweeps in, even the statues frozen …

In Marshall Fields
Under the Tiffany dome
The ladies come and go
Speaking of furnishings for home

"Johnny Nolan has a patch on his ass." Kids chase him through screen door summers. Somewhere a man laments upon a violin. A doorstep baby cries and cries again like a ball bounced down steps, which helps the afternoon arise again to a moment of remembered hysteria

And we played the Battle of Port Arthur in the tub and the water leaked down through the living room ceiling, and it was altogether too tragicomic, helpless laughter adding extra chords to the symphony still playing on the Victrola (all major chords happy, all minor chords sad)

*And she an infrared photographer*
                    *gave him an infrared look*
        *And he blinked his shutters*
                    *and was light-struck lovestruck*
                                        *ever after*
And she with her perfect teeth and deep cleavage
(claiming to be a deep-cleavage feminist)

Hope still a sign of where love might lie
The isolate human in the lonely crowd
Single mothers masturbating
next to sleeping kids

And he late at night hot for love
thinking back to his first love
and how she bared herself to him
But he so angel-struck
like Cherubino in *Le Nozze di Figaro*
he couldn't make a move on her
on Lulu Lulu
she of the hyacinth hair and naiad airs
in her West 12th Street studio
just out of Swarthmore
It was Lulu taught him how to "catalaya"
A la Proust and his Odette
and she hot to get married
but he too much a dreamer still
 (neither callow youth nor cocksman)
to know himself or to know her
or know what was Real
And she wandering off finally
to points west
drinking too much too long
and falling fatally down some winding stairs
somewhere in the farthest East
And he in love with her the whole time
(or so he thought)
*O Nymphea puidice Deum vidit, et erubuit*

A blink of an eye, and it's morning again. In winter coat and snap-brim hat, in wing-tip cordovan shoes and carrying a rolled umbrella and a box of the latest issue of *Big Table*, big Paul Carroll, looking like Buck Mulligan, editor and publisher of the afore-mentioned literary review, enters Barbara's Bookstore. Barbara herself places a copy of *Big Table* in her window. The mag has a patriotic red white & blue striped cover for its contents of beat rebel poetry banned by the University of Chicago (over which its student editors resigned and started *Big Table*).

Outside, a light rain descends on the city, silencing everything. It is as if silence itself were contained in the soft rain. Umbrellas blossom in it. There is a hush along the boulevards as it comes down. At the Chicago Art Institute silent couples under black umbrellas stroll out of Caillebotte's Paris and out onto the boulevard. They disappear in the rain sweeping in off Lake Michigan. The city sits silent, rooted, stretched like a huge octopus on the shores of the lake, its myriad eyes blinking, speechless. Its tentacles railroads....

So that—

　　　　the freights the long freights let out their shrieks in the Lake Erie dawn ... in fruit of first light ... their box cars strung out endless ... horizon to horizon ... engines disappeared westward and their tail ends still visible over the cornfields ... the corn itself stacked high in the open bins ... cradles rocking across America ... toward Huron ... Sandusky ... Port Clinton ... Toledo ... Admiral Perry offshore sends up his signal flags off Put-in Bay. The wind shifts and his flagship drifts. Becalmed in the middle-distance he's raked by British broadsides ... he rows to another ship carrying his flag with him.... He closes on the British brigs and blasts them with his cannonades ... and carries the day! The battle is won for Free Trade and all the Northwest Territory. And the freights roll on endless over the Territory ... over the empire ... past Lake Erie past Huron ... Cleveland to Detroit to Chicago.... And still the train cries out at crossings, red lights flashing, RR bell ringing, but at last here comes the end of it ... a ghost brakeman hanging out from the last platform of the last caboose ... railroad cap cocked up ... swinging his lantern. Still the train cries out, crying far away like the sea, sending its lonely signal to the good townsfolk, good burghers eating burgers, becalmed in backwaters of shopping malls and filling stations, and Admiral Perry still offshore, unsure of what bright future he was fighting for....

And life "goes on" ... with the populists and the socialists and the anarchists and the Chicago Surrealists ... and the Charles H. Kerr Publishing Company giving voice to them with many a brave book and pamphlet.

Dear Sid,
     It's been years and years since I took off for the Wild West but I had two vivid dreams of you this week——
               which must mean you are in the vicinity or that you are thinking of me somewhere.
     It's been so many years I have no idea where you might be living now, the last time I had an address for you was in Burlington, Vt., 
               and I have addressed this letter there, hoping somehow it will be forwarded, wherever you are.
     My address is on the envelope. It's the same. Ever since I came West I've stayed in this town.
               I'd love to hear from you and see you again and be with you again.
               Please write. Love—
                    the kid you knew as—*Danny Boy*

Dreaming of screen door summers
and family picnics in great meadows

*We were sailing along*
*on Moonlight Bay*
*You could hear the voices ringing*
*They seemed to say*
*You have stolen my heart, now don't go 'way*
*As we sang love's old sweet song*
*on Moonlight Bay*

On the walls of an old motel in Kenosha, Wisconsin, there's murals of Carthaginian warships on a blue sea. It could be Lake Michigan. All over the motel are shields and crossed spears, and the chandeliers look like medieval torture wheels. In the bar the mural shows ships with banks of rowers and ranks of crossbowmen aiming at each other. One trireme is tilted over. Ask the barmaid what these murals are supposed to represent, and she says, "The Shriners are big here. But Carthage weren't here first. It was two, three hundred miles away, in Illinois, and they done moved it here, includin' the Kissing Stone."
"So which is the real Carthage?" a guy asks her.
She eyes him. "You lookin' to pick a fight?"

And Nick Carraway remembering at the end of *The Great Gatsby* how he and Gatsby and Daisy were all from the West and it was all a story of the West, and he heading out himself, to where the Mississippi meets itself—

*Meet me in Saint Lo-eey Loo-eeee*
*Meet me at the Fair*

*Tell all the gals*
*I'll soon be there . . .*

And where the River Shannon flows into the Mississippi, young
O'Shanahan opening his pub. A far cry it was from the Liffey, but
he kept a proper place, he was a proper publican. Check yer guns
at the door—

*Never eat in a place called Mom's*
*Never play cards with a man called Doc*

Rivers the riparian corridors
for all creatures
man and not man
Down the rivers of windfall light
(not highways and freeways)
Dos Passos' Camera Eye
rolling over Chicago
and on along the forty-second parallel
skimming the landscape
first by birch bark canoe and stage coach
or by a low-flying plane
skimming the treetops
over waving plains of wheat
monstrous mountains and lost river valleys
sweeping over at tree-level
steering for democracy
or what?

# V.

While Alexis de Tocqueville saw the "Indians" crossing the river on
their Trail of Tears out of the Old South, men, women, and children
… with white priests "explaining hell to the savages…."

And Mark Twain emoting
"the basin of the Mississippi
is the Body of the Nation….
As a dwelling place for civilized man
by far the first upon our globe"

*Ah, how does Mother Mississippi flow through time …*

Listen
Says the river within you
Listen
to the voices of America
the voices of the people of America
(of the middle mind of middle America)
Away along a river run— all the way down—
Minnesota

Wisconsin
Iowa
Illinois
Missoura
Kentucky
Tennessee
Arkansas
Mississippi
Louisiana
all flooded down
all washed down
in heartland America

The river exists for coal
the river made of coal
"waist deep in the Big Muddy"
the people mired in it
and the further South you go the muddier it gits
with the other big rivers muddying into it
The Missouri, the Illinois, the Ohio....

All night myriad barges filled with great hills of coal
the mud of ancient epochs
Pushed by huge smoking tugs
steaming downriver
And endless coal trains
Night and day
trundling forever
up and down Ole Miss
All night they trundle
hundreds of cars long

up and down along the river
their lonely horns echoing in darkness
Iron Horses hooting far off
lost voices of America
carrying dirty coal
from the great coal basket of America

And on the radio channel
on the big tug frequency
voices with deep country accents
Twain's "back-country twang"
Captains and pilots yakking back and forth
as they pass each other on the river,
laconic, heavy with time,
telling what they've just passed
or what the other should look out for
filling the air with navigation lingo
depth of water ahead
where a barge went aground,
the exact location of so-and-so
or even offers to sell
"six thousan' foota whaate oak
settin' in ma back yar' outside Memphis
fifty cints a square foot
if ya want it come an' git it
Ah'll be home day afta tomara
Maane's the last house on tha lef' up the lane
Evabody kin faane it 'cept mah sista
who's been there fifty tames
and still cain't fine it" etc etc
Waist deep in the Big Muddy

The great river still here
in the dream of America
basin heart of America

But it ain't the river of Mark Twain's dream
the pre-coal river the ancient dreamin' river
Ask the river pilots and they'll tell you
The river towns all dying
all the way down
(home-towns boarded-up
all over America
stamped out by shopping malls
on nearby Interstates)

Trempealeau Wisconsin ("Dipped in the water") socked-in dense
fog. It's Saturday afternoon in the year two thousand and there's
a festival going on in the tiny town (the main street running to the
river) and a band playing old time jazz and folk and a grey man and
woman crooning to it and there's free hotdogs and popcorn and ci-
der and about a hundred old citizens sitting around in beach chairs
in the street and on the lawns, and then the man singing "There's
a star-spangled banner waving somewhere And when I die that's
where I want to beeee ..." and she's singing along kind of harmoniz-
ing in a granny voice, and a lot of kids with balloons run around in
the middle of the street, and a red balloon gets loose and takes off
into the deep sky and everybody goes "Awww!" and a raffle for a
plastic steamboat whistle in the old bar of the old old Trempealeau
Hotel where tourists are drinking vodka martinis while outside the
band is still playing and the sun is still setting over Ole Miss beyond
a banner on the shore reading "A Celebration so big it takes One
River and Four States to hold it!"

And on downriver at La Crosse Wisconsin a huge limestone Catholic cathedral deserted except for one penitent inside.

And bold headlands on downriver at Prairie du Chien, a bunch of miscellaneous mutts are barking on a dock at a cat on a raft And the sky goes suddenly dark with clouds from coal-burning power plants

And then Iowa and Guttenberg town with church steeples
and a Polka Mass going on in Saint Mary's Catholic church
Sunday morning with the liturgy sung to polka tunes—
"Come Now & Worship" sung to "Beer Barrel Polka"
"Gospel Acclamation" to "In Heaven There Ain't No Beer"
"Holy, Holy, Holy" ("Blue Shirt Waltz")
"Lamb of God" ("Liechtensteiner Polka")
The church jammed full, all-white, not a black or Latino in sight.

And Davenport, Iowa, a dying downtown and concrete malls over the horizon, with huge casinos afloat on the waterfront full of overweight people pulling slots (laws against gambling avoided by mooring a foot from shore) ... huge excursion paddle-wheel riverboats lighted up, floating cities in the night, all with steel hulls now that snags and deadheads can't punch a hole in, blasting casino tunes out of false calliope pipes with Indians in there reaping or losing Whitey's chips. And up little Main Street the old movie house with marquee boarded up and a deserted old Variety Hardware with three generations in the dark interior—grandmother father and mother and son all standing there waiting to sell a bolt of cloth or a saw or a single screw as the dusk drops down upon the river, the jugular vein of America.

And Tom and Huck and Big Jim seen
through the wrong end of the telescope
disappearing down river
Big black Jim
forever floating down it
toward what freedom ...

   *O sister let's go down let's go down*
        *down to the river to pray*
     *Come on brother let's go down*
         *down to the river to pray*
    *O father O father let's go down*
        *down to the river to pray*

   *Oh I went down*
    *down to the river*
     *down to the river to pray*
      *studying on the good old ways ...*

# VI.

Dark mind dark soul dark age
The peasant leads his horse through blackberry kingdoms
and comes out on a highway in the American West

So that—he the hero with a thousand facets
a walking storehouse of the past
appeared in his own dream
and spake in his inner ear
*I, Maximus, primo bullshitter,*
*I push on to the end*
*life a real dream*
*a pilgrimage*
*a labyrinth*
*a labyrêve*
*The street is dark*
*I shall stumble*
*in the empty ways of night . . .*

Oh he had seen it all
Heard it all

Heard coyotes in their dying call
Dingos wailing at the western wall
Jesuits praying in adobe
tolling the iron mission bell
*Sanctus Sanctus Sanctus Life is holy*

The 19th century ends
and turns into Highway 66
"the road of flight"
The myth haunts us
Prairie schooners into Pullmans
and the rutting continues
The night of the horse is over
It is the dawn after dreaming
and in the middle of the journey
we come upon our selves on a dark road
and recognize our selves for the first time
The lights come on
the country is electrified
the world lights up like a Ferris wheel
All the machines begin to hum
almost as it were in unison
Civilization beats out Eros
and Proust perishes
Gauguin escapes to Tahiti
as Tristes Tropiques
perish forever
A crowd flows over London Bridge
Westward
stick figures in the world's end
out of Giacometti

The Golden Hinde sails through the Golden Gate
and sets up as a tourist attraction
Sir Francis Drake's brass plate is dug up
and ends up in a glass case
in Bancroft Library Berkeley
The Tower of London is sold
and transported to Texas
Stout Cortez still astounded on a peak ...
A Passage to India
and an empire collapses
as Spengler shouts "I told you so!"
Chinese philosophers dreaming they are butterflies
drift up the Yangtse and disappear
as the sea continues its blind waves
Red tides reach up the Potomac
and paranoia floods the world
Drums drums drums Johnny Get Your Gun
In the morning still
a girl in a white linen dress
wearing a white picture hat
crosses Gatsby's lawn bright with promise
Gandhi dies but lives on
A Buddhist monk
immolates himself on-camera
*Sri Ram Jai Ram Jai Jai Ram*
Jesus on his Tree sticks up
signaling wildly

The rutting continues
"Strengthened to live Strengthened to die
for medals and positioned victories?"

"The world's an orphan's home"
Rootless polyglots roam the cities
spacecraft sweeping over
bearing short-haired Magellans in jumpsuits
as satellites sweep the earth
with high-resolution cameras
multiple fluid images
melding Minneapolis and Romania
Mississippi and Krishna
     *Hari rama hari rama Rama rama hari hari*
Fields and winds and waters
fog and birds and men
sweep the screen
and chase each other from it
The camera zooms in:
The Vietnam captain holds his pistol
to the peasant's head
It explodes in full color
on CBS ABC NBC
The world with its drums of blood
continues turning
The locust continues
to devour the world
Hunger persists
Love lurches on
listing to starboard
like a ship in a bottle
Human longing goes on
Loneliness a curse
Innocence persists
Ignorance persists

like a scratch on a TV window
like a scratch on a windshield
Twilight has no meaning
beyond the figurative
Lights burning in the night
the SS Queen Mary tied up forever
for tourists in Southern California
There is a soughing in the bilges …

Somewhere a naive figure
holds up a laurel wreath
a nymph a valkyrie a sybil
holds up a Golden Bough
Lovers still are riders to the sea
A horse comes alone from a torn village
*Ah love let us be true to one another*

Put a note in a bottle
like a schooner in a bottle
It'll survive the worst seas
Turner's shipwreck burning
off the Hook of Holland
Friend, an albatross wings above our land
It's a bird It's a man It's a plane
"Brightness falls from the air"
and the air burns
They used to call it a Darkling Plain
In the UN they are debating it
    *"It's still the same old story*
        *a fight for love and glory"*
A woman walks on the shore

Educated armies march over it
Life still an inn of joy and sorrow
Beloved come back
by any bridge
In the twilight holding up her skirts
Anna Livia stands
on the far strand at ebb-tide
"swept with confused alarms"
The air is shaken with light
The crickets begin again
on heavy summer nights
And everybody singing
around the campfire
> *There's a long long trail a-winding*
>> *Unto the land of my dreams*
> *Where the nightingales are singing*
>> *And the pale moon beams....*

# VII.

An adobe sun paints Route 66
Easy Riders over the asphalt
roar stoned into the sunset

Past Kell Robertson
beat cowboy poet drifter
with his beat-up guitar
and his weather-beat songs
on his Horse Called Desperation

And "the search for meanin'
leads through the dreamin'"
sang Tom Russell on the borderlands
with a settler tale to tell:
"An American primitive man
in an American primitive land"
"heard the sound of Indian drums
... heard the bugles blow
        before they rewrote history
            into a Wild West show"

"Gather round, you people,
Listen here and now, if you please
This land of yours was settled by
Bastards drunks and thieves"

And all those New York carpetbagger poets
"Angel-headed" in tight pants
(hard-ons showing)
heading westward on their Road
to Denver San Francisco and Mexico
leaving behind all those Manhattanites
who would never cross the Hudson
seeing still the *New Yorker* map of America
a great slough west of the Hudson
reaching all the way across
to palm trees on the Pacific
and Never Never Land in celluloid
with Chaplin and Garbo and Harold Lloyd

And Huck Finn Tom Sawyer's hero
leading the only free life
And on the last page of *Huckleberry Finn*
their hero Huck disappears forever
from their horizon
but lives on in the West
in a thousand photocopies
like Neal Cassady becoming Kerouac's Huck
the River turned into their Road
their souped-up car their raft
cruising America
like cowboy anti-heroes of American film
the eternal outsider

the hot rod his horse
hipster replacing liberated slave
high on freedom

And then Ti-Jean Kerouac
stoned on a rooftop in Mexico City
finding himself alone and lost
(and hip sociologists claiming
that his *Road* was the true tale
of the loss of American innocence)

So that—Cassady then becomes Ken Kesey's Huck
and Kesey (the Paul Bunyan of the Beats)
becomes Tom Wolfe's Huck

Voice of the Other America out there
The deep soul of America
lost in video game arcades and pinball machines
in suburban malls
where lived the lives
of the middle mind of America
in Legion Hall breakfasts
living room kaffeeklatsches
prairie primaries and church suppers
America America
the first hope and the final despair
reading between the lives—

*"Rancher Well-fixed*
*Wants young bride*
*ready to work and love.*

*French-speaker in the market for*
*business partner Out West"*

MUSIC THEORIST, multi-instrumentalist,
looking to form local band. Have horn, will travel.

FOR RENT: Single room, no drinking, no smoking, no visitors
after 10 PM, bathroom down the hall. CHEAP.

*WAKE UP SERVICE. Anytime Anyplace. Call only after 11 AM.*
*MAple 2-1010*

And the Great Plains stretching on forever
past where they drove that Golden Spike
with the hard labor of Chinese "coolies"

And on across Nevada
into Vegas
the City that Never Sleeps
past the huge electric sign that says

THE FATE OF THE WORLD DEPENDS
UPON THE WAY WE LIVE

And whiskey America plunges into the Soft Machine
Full of fear and loathing
*Hoc in terra Caesar est*

Jesus in dark glasses
on the bus to the Strip
carrying thirty pieces of silver

in a paper bag
In front of him an epileptic
in a gold golf cap
shaking his head continuously
uncontrollably
The silverhaired bus driver starts up
humming a tune from Naughty Marietta
We hum past
Tropicana Avenue    Lone Palm Motel
Shell Mobil    Private Pool Suites    Looney Tunes
HEAVEN    Funny Farm    Rent-a-Car    Solarcaine
Paradise Road Blue Chip Stamps    GOLF
Ice    Le Cafe    THE END    Drugs    HACIENDA
Mormon Temple    Towaway Zone    Coppertone
Gulf    Silver Slipper    Auto Refrigeration
Progressive Jackpots
Nevada Visitors Bureau
Penny Slots & Free Drinks    Las Vegas Boulevard
Play Nickels Win New Car    Hughes Air West
Bonanza Casino    Check Cashing Service
FOLIES BERGÈRE    "Never Before"    Sage & San
Hunt Breakfast    HOOVER DAM
"Old-Fashioned Hospitality"
Frontier Hotel
LAS VEGAS HILTON
THE DUNES
STARDUST
Westward Ho!
SHOWBOAT
FLAMINGO
DESERT INN

PYRAMIDS
CAESAR'S PALACE
Orange Julius
Our Marriage Chapel
Little Church of the West
"Thirty-Dollar Weddings"
"Go Home Satisfied or Refund"


Jesus Christ Superstar gets off
and rolls his eyes at the American Dream
that here begins again
on the Street That Never Sleeps
And "the extraordinary adventure of white America"
roars on
amid proofs it never experienced the Middle Ages
A huge cowboy on a hundred-foot horse
sits astride main street downtown
raises his neon Stetson
and says electronically
"Howdy, pardner"
His voice fills the air
his voice is everywhere
his picture printed in
The Voice of the Rockies
in the Desert News
with his daily horoscope:
"Scorpions are mystery men, violent and volcanic inside, de-
ceptively cool outside. They believe in revenge and vigorous
pursuit of women. The women among them make good spies, the
men good Mafia dons or police officers, either way, and superb
athletes. Let not Aries enter these premises."

Desert News sifts in like sand:
CLEVELAND MAFIA RULES VEGAS
"Geologists Say No Vegas Fault"
"Hearst's Daughter Castigates Hearst's America
Attacks 'Absolute Spiritual Bankruptcy'"
"People change in Vegas and become what they would like
to become and what they can't become back home"
"Who Is Not on the Hustle
In Life's Lottery?"

A covey of Oklahoma Mothers
with cowboy escorts
lands in The Blue Lagoon
A honeymoon couple from North Duluth
parks their blue Ford Phaeton
and struggles to the slots
Lady in the lobby in powder blue pants & clogs
sprays her hair with a blue spray can
talking on a lobby phone
"We come down here to a land sale.
We dint buy no land
but they give us free tickets
to everything!"
A Japanese student with a camera
scurries past to the john
A Sikh in a purple turban
is having trouble with his zipper
Slots whir in the Men's Room
PRESS BUTTON TO FLUSH
And out come the coins or condoms
A minister in blue

walks by jingling
a pocketful of dimes
Stands up to a slot
jiggles his pants
presses a button
and drowns in the
ELECTRONIC SHOOTING GALLERY
in the "Circus Circus":
"You're in the heart
of the deepest and darkest
jungles of Africa—
Step up
to the shooting counter, hunters—
pick up a gun, put a quarter in
the slot in front of you
and take careful aim—
"All the animals you hit
will scream, yell, move or holler—
Take your time
and hit all the red dots—
"Come in, hunters,
if you're brave enough to face
the dangers of the jungle,
pick up a gun
put a quarter in the slot
and start shooting—
"A deadly jungle killer
the black python
is hanging from a tree
waiting for someone
to make the wrong move—

"Watch the animals perform— Pick up a gun
and let them have it—
You get fifteen shots—
"On your left you see a native
with a blowgun—
When he's aiming at you
shoot him—
KLEAN OUT KIKES
KLEAN OUT WOPS
KLEAN OUT REDSKINS
KLEAN OUT SPICS
KLEAN OUT CREEPS
KLEAN OUT FREAKS
KLEAN OUT BLACK TRASH
"There once was a man
who sold the Lion's skin
while the beast still lived
and was killed
while hunting him"
and now
L'heure bleue
on the Strip
where time does not exist
except on the wrist of the dealer
and all that glitters is not gelt
and "behind the tinsel is the real tinsel"
in a Monopoly Game fantasy
dreamed up maybe by some Mormon Moloch
during the Great Depression
and stretched out there
in the great American desert

like some portable instant city
set down on the face of another planet
A five-mile long strip of jism
squeezed out like dry toothpaste on a cake

In desert dust storms
tumbleweeds
still blow
across Las Vegas Boulevard
and still will blow
after a river runs thru
Caesar's parking lot
with its cargo of dead cars
The Strip lights up
like a pinball machine
or a linear accelerator
brighter than the moon up close
the sky a neon ceiling
for a room inside a lightbulb
where it does no good to close your eyes
A helicopter from the Stardust Casino
moves the stars about
over the Appian Way
And the Roman legions come rolling
like a Rose Bowl Parade
with Caesar's Great Triumphal Car
drawn by six Percherons
hung with elephant bells
and leading Dürer's rhinoceros
on a string
There is a thrill in the air

The Roman legions come rolling
up to Caesar's Palace
Centurions
swing off their horseless chariots
parade up thru the gates
come to a halt & raise their visors
And look about
The face of the pit boss stares out
chewing the butt end
of a burned-out Havana
He raises his right arm
holds it like a salute
and brings it down with a crash
There is a whirring sound
His eyes light up and spin
with dollar signs in them
Like a lost plane
with feathered wings
The Winged Victory of Samothrace
has landed somehow
in front of
CAESAR'S PALACE
built by building trades and the Mafia
with union funds
Martial's Palatine Sonnet
quoted in the menu
And "Room Service a Roman Feast"
in the Frank Sinatra Suite
but no food served with Harry Belafonte
at the Midnight Supper Show
designed precisely to disgorge

the lushed-up masses
directly into the
carousel Casino
groaning with gaming tables
Roulette Baccarat Keno
in a sea of slot machines
one of which once in a while lights up
shakes all over
showers out Caesar's own silver dollars
and emits a puff of smoke

Whiskey America plunges in
into the Soft Machine
into the steaming pits
as into a burning landscape
painted by Gustav Doré
whose clouds were angels
Caesar not Virgil thy guide
Wearing blue and carrying a feather
will not win
Belafonte himself falls in
and drops $27,000 at Baccarat
and next night sings a song-cry
about the pit-bosses:
"If it moves and is warm
I will fleece it"
And at the baccarat tables
two dealers deal
the final Big Brother trip
And two pit bosses watch them
and three foremen watch the pit bosses

and one pit boss watches three foremen
from behind two-way mirrors
on the low ceiling
under which circulate the masses
mixed with house dicks
Hoc in terra Caesar est
The pudgy pit boss squats
on his highchair throne
rings on fat fingers
and a fat cigar clutched loose
a DeMille Caesar
with lizard looks watching wrong moves
Drear players with coin-eyes
stuck like horned toad zombies
round the board

"Phlebas the Phoenician, a fortnight dead"
holds his cards and hangs his head
Dawn breaks outside somewhere
and the deal continues
Gold sun bursts forth unseen somewhere
through a cottonwood grove
And the fast shuffle goes on
The walls themselves fall down
as in Buster Keaton movies
and they still play on
Pale Faces turning paler
impaled on rotating spits in pits
roasted with rotating oranges
apples & cherries
under glass

through which also wink & blink
Buffalo Heads & Indian Heads
in hock in terror in bas-relief
And Eisenhower eyes and Kennedy eyes
And the weird Third Eye that winks not
from its Transamerica Pyramid
in the dollar's green desert
And a scaled-down replica of Dante's Inferno
with Dante telling Virgil
"I had not known life had undone so many"
over which hangs a sign
WE NEVER CLOSE
in the land where make-believe makes believe

Where then it's time for the Great Cowboy
who became President
and rode to the Rio Grande
and gave the President of Mexico
a hunting rifle a bad omen
and how the Great Cowboy reconquered the West
and resettled Washington
and how the Metternich of Foggy Bottom still moved
behind the scenes
How they anointed generals to topple regimes
How the Great Cowboy ruled over all with a schoolboy grin
How his lady had a handgun with a pearl handle
How they gave human rights back to the wrong rulers
How they gave the land back to the old guarders
How the high rollers got back in the saddles again
How the Great Cowboy shook his head with a sheepish grin
for the benefit of a nation of sheep

How they buffaloed both sides
How they gave them bullets to bite
How they swallowed hard
when the Great Cowboy laughed on TV
How the Great Cowboy waved his hand
and disappeared over the horizon
How he walked softly and carried a big nuke
How he brandished it like a hunting rifle
How the President of Mexico gave him a great stallion
How he tried to mount it as the cameras rolled
How he slung his hunting rifle behind him and swung up
How the people hid in their houses
How the hot sun beat down on the mined land of the world
How the swinging door saloons stood empty and silent
How the natives were restless and beat their drums
How the Indians said "How come" instead of "How"
How the Great Smiler smiled no more on TV
How he came on his great white stallion
propped up from behind with a big stick
How he stood tall on the saddle
and looked straight into the cameras
How the old hands hid in the old corrals
How the deputies deputized themselves
and took to the roofs
How the people trembled in their houses
How they thought it was the final shoot-out
How a great hush fell upon the plazas of the world
And how the Great Cowboy put on one black glove
And how his eyes narrowed and his hand reached behind him
And how suddenly it was High Noon

"In the land that is utterly different from any other country"
this vast lonely, inchoate continent
where the loneliest road in America
(a sign on Highway 50 claims it)
cuts straight westward across Nevada
by Nightingale Hot Springs
where there never were no nightingales
among the grey cement power plant buildings
and the Kennecott Cortez Gold Mine
pumping out the virgin aquifer
Ancient salt lakes sucked up
to flush mine pits and injection ponds
in a cyanide heap-leach vat-leach operation
in a land Cortés never conquered
and Kennecott does it
At night the floodlights light up the deep pits
to the incessant sound of pumping
and the churning of giant earth-movers
with wheels as high as houses
destroying Indian earth and mountain
horizon to horizon
for a pickup load of gold
Mining towns once roaring
now shrunk to a railhead
Street lights stoned with loneliness
or lit with leftover sun
they drank too much of during the day
Trains hooting in the nowhere
Dingding crossroads flicker by
Homo sapiens on wheels …

Trains in the book of night!
across the great divides
across the inter-mountain country
over the purple plains
over the thirsty deltas
winding down at last
to the glowing Golden Gate....

# VIII.

So that—a certain young traveler, arriving overland by train to the San Francisco Embarcadero in the middle of the 20th century, shouldered his sea bag and set foot upon what he saw as some temporarily lost Atlantis risen from the sea. He saw the seven hills rising up in the early morning, with small white buildings sparkling in first light. The hills seemed to sing, and his step was light as he started up Market Street, breathing the bright air, uncertain what direction to take. And as he took in with hungry eyes the panorama of the City, he saw as never before the panorama of his own life stretched before him, with its unknowable possibilities, unfathomable, still hidden from him beyond the bright horizon. And like his hero, Stephen Dedalus, he thought to himself, "Welcome, oh life!"

*San Francisco! San Francisco!*
in that hinterland that stretches westward
all the way from Athens
Democracy! fighting through Dark Ages
medieval kingdoms bloody kings and dictators
to end up here at last
still an elite democracy?
with galley slaves in suits in skyscrapers?

And this truly the end of the line
the end of the long, long trail a-winding
 Land's End the Last Frontier
with no further West to go
the ideal place the final home
so longed-for over the Great Plains
over the Great Divide

After World War II
it was as if the whole continent tilted westward
and the population shifted with it
and it took almost a decade
for all the elements of a changed America
to come together
to coalesce
in a radically new post-war culture
And it happened in San Francisco

San Francisco! the radiant city,
with an island climate and an island consciousness
not really a part of the United States
a kind of off-shore colony
settled by adventurers prospectors drifters
fishermen castaway sailors and ladies of fortune
coolies card sharps and con men
everything but the good bourgeoisie
who moved in later and put up curtains

And San Francisco's 1906 earthquake & fire
inspired great plans to remap the whole city
a City Beautiful

with boulevards and plazas and cafes
a grand American Paris
But *gelt* ruled and it all ended up
shrunk to the northern waterfront
and the Panama-Pacific International Exposition
But great was the rejoicing in the City
risen like a phoenix from its ashes
for "this is what San Francisco always wanted to be"
Yet it lasted just nine months
and the City returned to its roots
as provincial capital
as working class city
polyglot social-democrats pacifists and anarchists
cheap wine and food in waterfront saloons
and workers' social clubs South of the Slot

And then the Preparedness Day Parade in 1916
organized by the Chamber of Commerce
to drum up patriotic support for the war
with organized labor opposition
a turning point in Labor history
with Tom Mooney and Warren Billings
framed for killing a cop
("Free Tom Mooney!" was the cry
until they were freed decades later)

And then Bloody Thursday July 15, 1934
in the great General Strike
of Longshoremen and seamen
a pitched battle between workers on one side
with thousands marching with them

and scabs and police against them
with Pathé News reporting it
in dreadful fearful tones
and shipping companies
from SF to San Diego
losing a million a day
as ships lay idle unloaded
their cargoes spoiling

So that—progressive San Francisco went on
through the Nineteen Forties and Fifties and Sixties
with the Longshoremen tying up the port
to protest Italy's invasion of Ethiopia
Fascist intervention in Spain's Civil War
and South Africa's apartheid
The city still an eccentric center of resistance
with counter-culture bookstores and newspapers raising hell
and KPFA radio founded by conscientious objectors
and Glide Memorial Church and the Mission Cultural Center
and Italian anarchists and the Bread and Wine Mission
and psychedelic poets and alcoholic figurative painters
and Utopian experiments and Diggers providing free food
and a commune that didn't use money
and back-to-the-land movements
tuning-in turning-on & dropping-out
and the Weather Underground
(its pamphlets appearing mysteriously
in bookstore basements)
And Bob Dylan singing "Masters of War" on KPFA

It is Sixties San Francisco
("Don't call it Frisco"
moaned columnist Herb Caen
because that's what riffraff sailors called it)
And the weight of the world
the weight of history
lies lightly on San Francisco
and all day long the light like early morning
that special San Francisco light

It is high noon everywhere
in the great American dream
with a rock dance in Longshoremen's Hall
and the very first light show
and the Jefferson Airplane takes off
and revs up the Summer of Love
and the Human Be-In
Timothy Leary and Richard Alpert
(later transformed into Ram Das)
psychedelically levitating a counter-culture
(with its own paper the San Francisco *Oracle)*
And it's "Be Here Now" and "Enlarge the area of consciousness"
The leading edge of the world-wave
to sweep around the world
A youth-revolt or youth-quake
(inspiring Paris '68)

"Stoned & singing Indian scat with Ravi Shankar
his sitar like a boat by the "river of life"
that flows on & on into "eternity"

Time itself a boat upon that river
Slow distant figures drawing barges
the small drum a pulse beating slow under the skin
And our bodies still in time transported
dreamt eternal by the Ganges—
a river still to be found in America ..."

While under the great trees at Ojai
Jiddu Krishnamurti
(who didn't want to be a guru)
emits pure light when he speaks
"It's all taking place in one mind"
On the lawn among the trees
lovers are listening
for the master to tell them they are one
with the universe or themselves
Eyes smell flowers and become them

In the Trieste Caffe the original beat hangout
where Gert Rude Stein
never said to J. Kerouac
"You are all a beat generation"
It's Saturday afternoon
with Italian family opera
the *bel canto*
so sentimental
so *antico*
in a hungry world
Papa Gianni singing his heart out
in "Granada"

And poet Kenneth Patchen
an e e cummings-with-an-attitude
saw the lonely people of the world
even as he made love to Miriam
(love of all his days)
Voice of the conscience of the world
defiant to the end of his bedridden days
the anti-hero singing in the suburbs
And Kenneth Rexroth
the resident godfather of the poets
waxing wroth about capitalism
"the enemy of democracy"
And Martin Luther King repeating
"We are on the wrong side of the world revolution"

In this country where they assassinate their leaders
(as barbaric as the Aztecs)
and their stars kill themselves …

In San Francisco it's the Summer of Love
and the sound of Rock
hits Bill Graham's Fillmore Auditorium
drowning out cool jazz
And then the Last Waltz of Dylan's band
on the day that Winterland closed forever
brings the Sixties to an end
sometime in the Seventies
although VW busses painted with rainbows
and signs reading "Further" still rocked on.

It is still high noon everywhere in America
and it ain't the old worn out Europa
with Pier Paolo Pasolini writing in his journal
"The disappearance of fireflies in Italia
signals the start of a terrible era"

And loneliness still a blight
Ginsberg cruising Kansas highways
In his "Fall of America"
loveless in his public solitude
While lonely Jack from Lowell writes to himself, "I dedicate
myself to myself, my loneliness, my unique madness, my endless
absorption and hunger—because I cannot dedicate myself to any
fellow being…."

Yet even he Jean-Louis de Kerouac
of the Lowell *canuck* Kerouacs
had loved a woman deep

    *And one time for a moment*
        *His eyes met hers*
    *And he gazed*
        *Into the loveliest of minds*

And on a bar's new tv
a great black man boxing and singing
    *Float like a butterfly*
        *Sting like a bee*
            *I am Muhammad Aliiiiii*

While on a tin cup corner
a beat-up old lady
her face a wrung-out rag
(O happy he
    who held those breasts
      apples of bliss
        purely hanging
          once upon a time)
stumbles across the street
looking for butts
Old bag of blood
with a history to tell
of where all that blood came from
coursing through generations of generations
through her children and lovers
All those swimming unsinkable genes
in veins and arteries of the world
sailing through rife humanity
through that broken body
A walking gene pool
teeming tide pool born of oceans
repository of the past
Mother of us all

    *Desiring only my head*
    *Between your breasts—*

And a woman telephoning
On her cell phone on a street corner—
Private lives he'd never know!

nor sleep with
nor know their longings

And the #15 bus comes groaning along
                 loaded with all of humanity
Old Chinese woman with lampshade hat
            waddles across the street in time to catch it
Woman in front seat with a mutt in a basket says
        "But he's a terrier and knows a lot of words …"
"Mostly swear words," mumbles her guy.

The bus lurches on
into the eternity of here and now
The light changes and the world rushes by

And a junkie taxi driver
leans back to tell his fare
"Television's leadin' us straight to Nothin'"

While at the Ferry Building facing the bay
a ferry arrives and disgorges its morning crowd
into the City that holds so much promise
with its white buildings rising up and up
And despair and desire are seated on a bench
where a young woman is weeping
The sun shines down on her
and more ferries arrive
disgorging more humans
as the sun continues shining
as she continues weeping
and gets up finally and vanishes
into the radiant morning

*A quiver pierced my heart*
*When she went by*
*How and why could this stranger*
*Do that to me*
*Was she some mother to me*
*Lost in infancy*
*Her look by chance*
*a long lost glance*
*from eye to eye in me*
*a bell a distant singing . . .*

It was still high noon in America
until along came the digital revolution
fated to destroy or ingest
all the age-old cultures
of the world
in a World Wide Web
of globalization
in an Ayn Rand projection
of world domination


While out on San Francisco Bay
the yachts the white yachts
with their white sails in sunlight
catch the wind and heel over
All together racing now
for the white buoy
to tack about to come about beyond it
and then come running in
before the spanking wind
white spinnakers billowing
off Fort Mason by the Golden Gate

where once drowned down
an Alcatraz con escaping
his bones turned to sand
fifty fathoms down
and still imprisoned there
in the glass of the sea
As the so skillful yachts
freely pass over

While on a dark corner downtown
a dude in a downtown suit
is about to pass a black dude
who's trying to sell the *Street Sheet*
put out by the Coalition for Homelessness
The suit stops in front of him
And blurts, "Why're you doing this?"
The black man rears back
"You got no right!
You got no right to ask
until you stood in my shoes!
You got no right
'til you been to a war and back
like I did.
You come back and stand in my shoes!"
The suit presses on—
"I just want to understand why—"
"Nevehmind! You got no nevehmind!
You got no right!"

He saw one of them sleeping huddled under cardboard
by the Church of Saint Francis

He saw one of them rousted by the priest
He saw one of them squatting in bushes
He saw another staggering against the plate glass window
of a first class restaurant
He saw one of them in a phone booth shaking it
He saw one with burlap feet
He saw one in a grocery store come out with a pint
He saw another come out with nothing
He saw another putting rope through the loops of his pants
He saw one with a bird on his shoulder
He was one of them singing on the steps of City Hall
in the so cool city of love
He was one of them trying to give a lady cop a hug
He saw another sleeping by the Brooklyn Bridge
He saw another on the Golden Gate
The view from there was great.

While at the stoplight waiting for the light
Nine A.M. downtown San Francisco
a bright yellow garbage truck
with two garbage men in red plastic blazers
standing on the back stoop hanging on
and looking down into an elegant open Mercedes
with an elegant couple in it
and both scavengers gazing down
as from a great distance
at the cool couple
as if they were watching some odorless TV ad
in which everything is always possible
And the very red light for an instant
holding all four close together

across that great gulf between them
in the high seas of their democracy

And out on the city's first freeway
people in steel cabinets on wheels
hightailing it
Five PM Friday rush hour
They're escaping
almost flying

Home to the nest
home to the warm caves
in the hidden hills & valleys
home to daddy home to mama
home to the little wonders
home to the pot plants behind the garage
The cars the painted cabinets
streak for home home home
home to their own democracy
THRU TRAFFIC MERGE LEFT
home to the hidden turning
the hidden yearning
home to San Jose
home to Santa Cruz & Monterey
home to Hamilton Avenue
home to the Safeway the safest way
yield
left lane must turn left

Home to the little grey home in the West
home to Granddaddy on the golf course

home to Uncle Ned
puttering in the toolshed
having lost his pants
on the stock exchange
home to big sister
who lost her way in encounter groups
home to the 97-lb housewife
driving two tons of chrome & steel
three blocks to the supermarket
to buy a package of baby pins
home to little sister
blushing with boyfriends
in the laundry room
home to kid brother with skateboards & Adidas
home to mad Uncle building CB radios
in hidden bunkers
home to backyard barbecues
with aerospace neighbors
Mr. Wilson's coming over
The Hendersons will all be there
Home to Hidden Valley
where the widow waits
by the Cross on the mountain
where hangs the true madness
home to Santa's Village
WILL DIVIDE TO SUIT
GAS FOOD LODGING NEXT RIGHT
home to where the food is

Home to Watsonville
home to Salinas

past the Grapes of Wrath
past United Farmworkers
stooped over artichokes
home home over the horizon
where the sun still blows
into the sea
home to Big Sur
as the sun sets in lavender skies

Home sweet home the salesman sighs
home safe at home in the bathroom
safe with the washing machine & dishwasher
safe with the water heater
safe with the kitchen clock
tick tick
the time is not yet
the alarm is set
safe at last in the double bed
hidden from each other
in the dark bed by the winding stair
the enchanted place in the still air
hidden each from each
or the queen-size bed the king-size bed
the waterbed with the vibrator
with the nylon nympho in it
the bed with Big Emma in it
with the stoned-out Angel in it
(Mountains of flesh
Hills of hips & thighs
Groans & moans & cries!)
Home to the bed they made

and must lie in
with "whoever"
Or home to the bed still to be made
of ragas & visions
the bed whose form is pure light
(and unheard melodies
dark despairs & ecstasies
longings out of reach)

Who to decipher them who answer them
singing each to each?
Hidden from themselves
The beds are warm with them
The bedsprings quake
on the San Andreas Fault
The dark land broods
Look in my eye, look in my eye
the cyclops tv cries
It blinks and rolls its glassy eye
and shakes its vacuum head
over the shaken bodies
in the bed

PENINSULA LIVING not for this virile man
looking for SF home with playmate. #r3786592

STRAIGHT MALE seeks settled life with loving womb
Anywhere in SF. LTR to ex#3476985

Divorced, trans gen, looking for home
life with new partner. LTR. ex#922212

*There's the friendly town of Loveland*
                    *Beside a lake of blue*
        *with mountains in the distance*
                    *Sending love to you ...*

TESTOSTERONE BLOWOUT!
*HOT VISUALS!*
*PULSATING BEAT & HEAVY BREATHING*
*WORSHIP AT THE ALTAR OF THE GREAT PISTOL!*
*GET YOURS!!!*
(Private Viewing Booths)

*Dear Sis ..... Upon returning from Minnesota frozen north and reading the lonely Swedish poet Tranströmer I realize loneliness is still growing all the time in this country—an enormous loneliness still all over America—and perhaps soon that will be all that's left in the world—which was always there perhaps—an existential loneliness that's at the root of everything, and it keeps growing, and I will have to grow too, to keep up with the growing loneliness and not shrink away into nothingness myself, or else loneliness will fill up my whole room, and nothing be left outside of me except the demon of loneliness who grows all the time because he doesn't want to be alone in an empty furnished room, with pee-stains on his underwear, like Gregory Corso said in his poem about getting married. It occurs to me that I am that loneliness itself and that I have a terror of myself always growing larger and larger and more lonely, so that eventually I will be the last person I know on earth and everyone else strangers, and maybe that is the fate of all the very very old, and maybe this final loneliness doesn't actually happen until the day of death and then the corpse fills the whole room?*
        *—Love—Me*

Remembering speechlessly
the great forgotten language,
the lost lane-end into heaven....


*Louise, Louise ....... How shall I address you now, after all this
time! How many lives have we lived and lived and lost and passed
on since back then? It's like, when we came West, we crossed some
Great Divide, never to go back, to our former lives or selves, as if,
as if ..... Oh, I don't know.... I only know I must see you again,
someplace, somehow, if only for a few moments. I need some kind of
closure.... Oh, there must be some other way for us to exist, except
apart, wandering like this.... Shall I call?——A*

But the War against the Imagination
Is not the only war
And the Death of the Imagination
Not the only death that counts ...

# IX.

The forest fires of the Kali Yuga
about to consume us
 and Smokey the Bear
in his broad Park Rangers hat
in his raging fury
to save planet earth
still swings his vajra-shovel
to douse the fires of greed and war
and still chants his great enlightened mantra

*But who hears it*
 *as it echoes in the wilderness?*

With the forced march of Progress
forcing all onward
Technocracy versus the heart
The aristocracy of corporations
versus the People
Macrotiendas in Teotihuacan
The pyramids lit up like cupcakes

Capitalism masquerading as democracy
"with free speech only
for those who have nothing to say"
and carrying within itself
the seeds of its own destruction
(and all the other clichés of the Left)

*"I heard the news today Oh boy . . ."*

Man too stupid and too greedy
to save himself from eco-catastrophe?
in an Armageddon of autos
in the City of Angels
in downtown Denver
in Chicago and Manhattan
Mexico City and Milan
Calcutta and Tokyo
drowned down in the bad breath of machines
The sun's wearing shades
the ozone layer breathing smog
The ecosystem as finely balanced as a mobile sculpture
A computer about to crash
A casino culture out of control
A hole in its ozone soul
A sweepstakes Winner Take All
A shooting gallery
for masters of war
A bull market with toreadors
A runaway juggernaut heading for naught
A runaway robot bombing through cities
The hydraulic brakes blown
Internet gamblers and dot-com billionaires

Coked-up in stretch limos
and Martin Luther King saying
It's now up to us to choose
non-violence or non-existence

The whole spinning world lights up
*TILT!*
A billion jackpots blow with a bang
*"Kingfishers catch fire*
*Dragonflies draw flame"*
Shoppers carried by escalators
into the flames
Skin-deep civilization
gone in a flash of samsara
as the carbon air bursts into flame

*Rockabye, baby*
Swing low, sweet chariot
into the far future
when nations and borders no longer exist
and a *great swarming* of fellaheen hordes
sweeps the earth
in search of food and shelter

The leadsman takes his soundings
and cries aloud "Mark, twain!"
as the lead-line plunges down....

And so *sic transit* the glories
of our century

In our time of useful consciousness

Enough! Enough!
Enough of this "loud lament of the disconsolate chimera"
in some waste land of our impoverished imagination.

Did not Martin Luther King have a dream
and did he not opine
that "only when it's dark enough
can you see the stars"?

We still can cry "Abandon all despair!"
for we still have our "lyric escape"

Oh let us see again
with dreamy poet Yeats
"The silver apples of the moon
The golden apples of the sun"

Oh let us all croon at the moon
in full denial!

> *Bye bye blackbird blackbird blackbird*
> > *singing the blues all day*
> *Bye bye blackbird*
> > *why you say*
> > > *there ain't gonna be*
> > > > *no sunshine no more*
> *Blackbird blackbird*
> > *Gotta be on my way*
> > > *Where there's sunshine all a day*

How lovely still the earth
and all the creatures in it
shining in eternity
as the sun
the sun so bright
shakes out its golden hair
of streaming light

*And are there not still fireflies*
*Are there not still four-leaf clovers*
*Is not our land still beautiful*
*our fields not full of armed enemies*
*never occupied*
*by iron armies*
*speaking iron tongues*
*Are not our warriors still valiant*
*ready to defend us*
*Are not our senators*
*still wearing fine togas*
*Are we not still a great people*
*Is this not still a free country*
*Are not our fields still ours*
*our gardens still full of flowers*
*our ships with full cargoes*
*Is not Rome still Rome*
*Is not Los Angeles still Los Angeles*
*Are these really the last days of the Roman Empire*
*Is not beauty still beauty*
*And truth still truth*
*Are there not still poets*
*Are there not still lovers*

*Are there not still mothers*
            *sisters and brothers*

*Does not a dawn every day*
*still light up our land*
*Is there not still a full moon*
                    *once a month*
*Are there not still fireflies*
*Are there not still stars at night*
*Can we not still see them*
            *in the bowl of night*
                    *signalling to us*
                        *some far-out*
                            *beatific destiny?*

Walt Whitman, you should be living at this hour!
Optimist of humanity *en masse*
Old greybeard—old Walt
stepping off Brooklyn Ferry
into the heart of America—
You who contained multitudes
You who heard America singing
You who sounded your barbaric yawp
 over the roofs of the world
You who said "I'll whimper up no more"
 Out of the closet endlessly rocking
You who struck up for a New World
"Solitary, singing in the West"—

*Whereaway now, dear poet, dear lover, eternal yea-sayer?*

————END————

# NOTES

A fragmented recording of the American stream-of-consciousness, in the tradition of William Carlos Williams' *Paterson*, Charles Olson's *Maximus*, Allen Ginsberg's *Fall of America*, and Ed Sanders' *America: a History in Verse*.

"Time of Useful Consciousness," an aeronautical term denoting the time between when one loses oxygen and when one passes out, the brief time in which some lifesaving action is possible. (The phrase is used as the call letters of TUC RADIO, an FM broadcaster, produced by former KPFA/Pacifica Radio staffer Maria Gilardin.)

Certain separate poems previously published are here given a context.

1/1/12